SØREN KIERKEGAARD

by

ROBERT L. PERKINS

JOHN KNOX PRESS

Atlanta

British edition published by the Lutterworth Press
4 Bouverie Street, London, England, 1969

American edition published by John Knox Press
Richmond, Virginia, 1969

Library of Congress Catalog Card Number: 69-14337

International Standard Book Number: 0-8042-0710-0

Second Printing 1976

Printed in the United States of America
John Knox Press
Atlanta, Georgia

Contents

Introduction

WILLIAM OF OCKHAM employed the principle of parsimony or economy. It is popularly called 'Ockham's razor' and states that entities must not be multiplied without necessity. Without this principle it would be impossible to understand the rise of the modern sciences, both natural and social. Ockham's discussion of the principle is very closely related to the development of nominalism in philosophy and empiricism in science.

Kierkegaard developed the principle of parsimony in the direction of theology. Not every theological notion is of equal importance and not everything needs to be mentioned. It would perhaps be too much to say that he reduces theology to Christology, but all issues are clarified in the light of the central meaning of Christ and the incarnation. Even his understanding of the human condition is derived from this source.

Kierkegaard rejected the notion of theological system and never wrote a systematic theology. Even the topics he treated are discussed in a non-systematic and indirect fashion. Kierkegaard found that existence is fragmentary, unsystematic, sometimes even absurd, and could not be reduced to a philosophic system. In the same way, the central notions in Christian theology, such as the incarnation, cannot be contained under any ordinary concept of reason. The incarnation states that God in Jesus Christ was flesh, and this appears to be an irrational mixing of the human and divine categories. It is also possible that there would be factors other than reason militating against acceptance of the incarnation.

Furthermore, he frequently thought that aside from logical problems involved in the concept of theological systems, the systems tended to be pompous and verbose ; to answer questions which people were not asking ; to emphasize the unessentials, making them as prominent as the essential ; and to breed intellectual mediocrity. Kierkegaard insisted that theology must always be dedicated to rethinking itself in the new categories of each succeeding age. This rethinking itself does not mean that the gospel changes, but only that theology must change. System, on the other hand, suggests completion.

Systematic thinking also tends to become a substitute for acting on the truth. Truth is something that must be gained by each man, and gained time and again, and must become the basis of his life. Truth itself is not a finished system but is in a process of becoming like the subject who acts on the basis of it. This new way of looking at the nature of truth forced Kierkegaard to re-examine every philosophic and theological category and to emphasize a new dimension of truth, that of its relation to the human subject.

A second-hand, acceptable and accepted system of religious truth leads to unthinking sincerity of belief and practice at best and to mediocrity at worst. Kierkegaard is sufficiently a rationalist to realize that sincerity and mediocrity are not a substitute for radical, searching thought and committed action. 'Evil, mediocrity, is never so dangerous as when it is dressed up as *sincerity*.'[1] Kierkegaard invites one to a feast of radical rethinking of the theological heritage and not to a stale meal of warmed-over systematic pottage.

Although Kierkegaard used Ockham's razor to eliminate the systematic domination of theological thinking, we must exercise the same instrument on his work. Here we shall consider only the theological thrust of three works, the *Philosophical Fragments*, *The Concept of Dread*, and *The Sickness unto Death*. The first two Kierkegaard thought of as companion pieces and the last supplements *The Concept of Dread*. The *Fragments* shows the theocentric focus of Kierkegaard's thought, and the last two, the anthropocentric. It is our hope to elucidate the resulting dialectic.

[1] Dru, Alexander, *The Journals of Søren Kierkegaard*, 1035.

My thanks are due to Professor Howard Hong of St. Olaf College, the editors of the series, Miss Beverly Stewart, my student assistant, and my wife Clarise for many suggestions which considerably improved the text.

I

Life

ALL too often the philosophic and theological merit of
Kierkegaard's work has been judged adversely because
of his peculiar psychological make-up. That is a genetic
fallacy. Most of his works were to some extent generated by his
reflection on important events of his life, but their significance is
independent of the facts related below. By means of irony,
humour and dialectic he was able, like Socrates, to transmute
these events into a philosophical position of considerable import.

Kierkegaard was born on May 5, 1813, in Copenhagen.
His childhood was quite unusual. The principal reason for this
was his father, Michael Pedersen Kierkegaard, a shrewd business-
man who retired at the age of forty to spend the remainder of
his days in reading philosophy and theology, debating with
professors whom he frequently invited to dinner at the home,
and disputing with any and all. But this argumentative man was
much more than a dilettante in philosophy and theology, a
shrewd dialectician and gracious host. He was a man who had
an intense burden of guilt which reached back to his childhood.
One rainy day on the top of a little hill when he was a child, cold,
lonely, and hungry, keeping someone else's sheep on the heaths
of Denmark, he shook his fist at the sky and cursed Almighty
God who had made him such a miserable creature. After this
event things went better and the child became the man and the
man became prosperous. Though most of us would tend to
think such material prosperity the blessing of God, he felt that
it was a divine curse upon him, and became morose, lonely, and
guilty in his inner life.

A second reason why Kierkegaard's father carried this burden
of guilt was that a few months after his first wife died giving

birth to a stillborn child, the housemaid gave birth to a child.
The assumption is that he had either seduced or raped her while
his wife was pregnant. The realization that he was a man capable
of such a deed greatly increased his burden of guilt. He married
the woman and she became the mother of all his children, of
whom Søren was the youngest.

Kierkegaard was the most frail physically, the most brilliant
intellectually, and the apple of his father's eye. He was the
Joseph of the family, specially loved by his father, who gave him
many hours of private instruction and took him for long walks
through the city and drives through the country. In bad weather
they used to walk up and down the front room of the house on a
journey to any place. The father with his brilliant imagination,
his keen sense of observation and his detailed descriptions, made
these trips more entertaining than the real trips through the
countryside or the city. In this way they could journey through
the whole world in an afternoon. Obviously these two were
made for each other and their fates were bound up together.

Kierkegaard began school in 1821 and did quite well, but he
had his problems there. He declared that he was 'infinitely
pugnacious' all his life. He was the object of some ridicule
because his father, though wealthy, insisted that clothes should
be worn out and Kierkegaard wore hand-me-downs. Some of
his fellow-students also ridiculed his awkward posture, the way
he walked, and his smallness. On these occasions they had good
cause to regret their temerity.

Kierkegaard's performance in school was outstanding. He
had a deep love of the Latin language, and his Greek was good
also. He mastered the main elements of the humanistic education
required in the gymnasium of the day. The intellectual stimula-
tion and the education begun there was a foundation of his whole
life's work.

Having finished at the gymnasium, he matriculated at the
University of Copenhagen in October, 1830. His father had
determined that he should be a priest in the Lutheran state
church, but after a year at the University Kierkegaard was just

as determined not to be a priest. Relations with his father went from bad to worse, with the result that Kierkegaard left home and moved into his own lodgings in 1837. His father settled sufficient funds upon him, but away from his father's influence he became rather a spendthrift.

Kierkegaard apparently was only wasting his time in the University. He appeared to be simply the perpetual non-student absorbing what he could but not making any real progress in the serious business of earning a degree and getting on in the world. Nevertheless, he was well-liked and was closely associated with all the students who later came to positions of leadership in the country. After several months' estrangement from his father, they were reconciled about a year before the father died. He never moved back home, but kept various lodgings in the city, moving only a time or two during the rest of his life. The death of the father was a grievous blow to Kierkegaard, and yet it was some relief because several of the children had died before their father and it had become a superstition between Kierkegaard and his father that all the children would die before they reached thirty-one and before the father himself. Now that his father was dead, Kierkegaard had mixed emotions—relief, guilt and love.

After his father's death, Kierkegaard faced the serious question of what he would do with his life. Though he certainly had money enough to live a normal life without having to work, he felt he could not go about doing nothing. Convinced by his deceased father's arguments, he began to study for his theological examination which he passed with honours in July, 1840. He then decided to prepare a dissertation for the master's degree which he defended with credit and honour to himself on September 29, 1841. The title of the dissertation, *On the Concept of Irony with Constant Reference to Socrates*, contains two ideas which followed him until the end of his life : *irony* and *Socrates*.

While Kierkegaard was preparing for his theological examination and writing his master's dissertation, he courted a young girl by the name of Regina Olsen. Regina was only sixteen, and

Kierkegaard had to overcome considerable opposition from the family and from a rival for her affections. In fact, at the time that he started courting her she was already engaged to one Fritz Schlegel. Kierkegaard won the affections of the family. Since he was courting Regina in a covert manner, he never expressed the slightest criticism of Fritz but rather emphasized his sterling character, fine wit, his exciting and likeable personality, as well as the fine figure he cut in the town. This was not the rather lacklustre Fritz known to the family, and in exasperation Regina finally broke the engagement.

Kierkegaard now found the field open and he simply swept Regina off her feet. On September 10, 1840, they announced their engagement. However, the very night the engagement was announced, Kierkegaard discovered that he was much happier thinking about her, writing a letter to her, writing a poem about her, than in her physical presence. In fact, he found her physical presence so much excess baggage. Kierkegaard knew that he had made a mistake : he had fallen in love with love.

If he broke the engagement, this would lead to her everlasting shame and she would probably never be able to marry. Furthermore, serious doubts regarding his melancholy arose as to whether he could ever marry. The only thing he thought he could do was to create a situation in which she could break the engagement. It was tortuous for him, and yet at the same time it was a proof of how deeply he loved her and what a high regard he had for the marriage vows. Whereas he had courted this girl with vivacity, sweetness and tenderness, he now became bitter, shrewish and harsh. Both suffered tremendously. The father, a proud man who was a judge in the town, asked Kierkegaard to marry her. Finally, after several months, she broke the engagement on October 11, 1841. Kierkegaard was now all too well known in the town, but for the wrong reasons. After a few days he departed on the first of his three trips to Berlin.

In Berlin he attended the lectures of Schelling who had been recommended to him by a Danish student. At first he was enthusiastic about Schelling but finally he became so disappointed he concluded that Schelling would dribble on to the end of the age. He had opportunity to hear Trendelenburg, but badly advised by one of his Danish fellow-students he never attended Trendelenburg's lectures—much to his later regret. Otherwise he enjoyed Berlin very much . The first week in March he returned from Berlin suddenly on hearing that Regina was ill, but upon his arrival in Copenhagen he learned the illness had not been serious.

In February 1843 he began to publish the works laboriously written during the months since the breaking of the engagement. This was the beginning of the pseudonymous literature which was to play such an important role in Kierkegaard's reputation. The initial series ended in February 1846. During these years he published *Either/Or*, *Fear and Trembling*, *Repetition*, *The Concept of Dread*, *Philosophical Fragments*, *Stages on Life's Way*, and *The Concluding Unscientific Postscript to the Philosophical Fragments*. These were published under various pseudonyms but at the end of the *Postscript* Kierkegaard declared himself the author of the whole series. These books were accompanied by another series of books published under his own name, which had the character of edifying discourses and were offered as foils to the pseudonymous writings or as expressions of his innermost religious convictions at the time.

Kierkegaard thought the *Postscript* would be literally concluding and he was considering seeking a country parish. However, at this time another momentous event occurred in his life. While he was reading the proofs of the *Postscript*, the *Corsair*, a somewhat indelicate and satirical journal, reviewed *Either/Or* and praised it. Kierkegaard felt that the *Corsair* was a detriment to Danish society, and therefore he asked in a public letter that he should not be the only one made immortal by the praise of the *Corsair*. As a result of this request, Kierkegaard was caricatured, criticized, lied about, and vilified in the pages of the *Corsair* for nearly a year. This made a deep impression upon him. The attack from the *Corsair* cut him off from many of the people he valued most—the children and the working man.

He had felt that respectable society which had been the constant object of the *Corsair*'s laughter would come to his rescue ; instead, he was merely dropped from the invitation list to the best parties, dinners and social occasions. We cannot appreciate at this distance how deeply such an enforced isolation hurt Kierkegaard, but his internal suffering was severe.

The *Corsair* affair finally turned out as Kierkegaard wanted. The editor, Meir Goldschmidt, upon learning the deep hurt he had inflicted upon Kierkegaard, closed the magazine and left Copenhagen in October, 1846, for over a year. Kierkegaard had an apparent, though costly, victory from which he learned a great deal. The suffering and isolation he endured during this time contributed to the clarification of his understanding of innocent suffering and of the Christian's heterogeneity with the world.

In the years that immediately followed the *Corsair* affair he published the *Works of Love*, *Edifying Addresses in Various Spirits*, *Christian Discourses*, *The Lilies of the Field and the Birds of the Air*, *The Sickness unto Death*, *Training in Christianity*, *The Gospel of Suffering* and *For Self-Examination*. These works were more and more clearly Christian in nature. The only exception to the religious quality of the works of this period was *A Crisis and the Crisis in the Life of an Actress*. Two other important works were written during this period but were not published during his lifetime : *The Book on Adler* and *Judge for Yourselves!* In these works he finally came to clarify and to delineate his conceptions regarding Christian theology as a whole and the concept of 'Christian' society.

In the years immediately following, from around 1850–1855, Kierkegaard published very little. He wanted to be silent and end his life without direct criticism of the state church or Christendom as he knew it. However, as one now reads the last mentioned works one realizes that his thought was on a collision course with bourgeois Christianity in the nineteenth century in general and with the Danish state church in particular. During this time Kierkegaard accumulated a great deal of material in his journals of a polemical nature against the church and Christendom which he hoped he would never have to publish. Yet, as time passed he saw more and more the necessity of entering into direct and open criticism of the church through the public press. This is a remarkable change on Kierkegaard's part, because throughout his life, and particularly since the affair with the *Corsair*, he had been suspicious of the press. The occasion which precipitated his attack on the church was the death late in 1853 of J. P. Mynster, an old family friend and bishop of Zealand.

As part of the memorial to Bishop Mynster, Hans Larsen Martensen, Kierkegaard's old theological professor, preached a sermon in which he eulogized Bishop Mynster as 'one more link in the holy chain of witnesses for the truth stretching from the days of the apostles into our own times'. This characterization of Bishop Mynster, Kierkegaard thought, was a falsification of every Christian category. Furthermore, Bishop Mynster was wealthy whereas the Son of Man had no place to lay His head ; he was an official of the state whereas Christ suffered under Pontius Pilate ; he was well respected in his community whereas Christ had been rejected of men.

Kierkegaard began to publish his attack on the church, but just as he was sending the first article to *The Fatherland*, a nationalistic newspaper, he realized that Martensen wanted to be bishop. Kierkegaard, either from good will or from the hope he could still avoid the attack, held up its publication until Martensen was confirmed as bishop. He then sent the first of twenty-one articles to the paper, which were published irregularly from December 1854 until May 1855. Beginning in May and continuing until his death in November, he published his own little sheet, *The Instant*. Martensen tried to reply once in the papers but his reply only indicated that he did not understand the issues. Numerous people misunderstood the attack on the church as an attack on the character of Bishop Mynster whom Kierkegaard had honoured in life as a friend. Nothing could be farther from the truth. The attack was against Christendom in general and Protestantism in particular ; especially against the watered-down,

B

unchristian, middle-class accommodating Protestantism of nineteenth-century Denmark. However, it was all soon to end.

In October, 1855, Kierkegaard fell in the street paralysed. He was carried to Frederick's Hospital where he lingered for about a month. The last month of his life was no easier than the rest because well-meaning people tried to get him to take it all back, to recant, but he would not. He refused the last sacrament from a clergyman with the demand that it should be sent by a layman—one who was not a flunkey of the state. Kierkegaard died on November 11, 1855.

But his death was not the end of the notoriety. No sooner was he dead than it came to light that a well-organized funeral had been planned. The funeral was held a few days later with Kierkegaard's brother, Peter, apologizing for Kierkegaard. The church was crowded, and when the interment took place at Assistens-kierkegaard on the outskirts of the city, the student body of the University created some little ruckus about the way the whole thing had been handled.

His works always contained some irony and were as prickly as Socrates. In the last attack the irony disappeared, but the Danish gadfly was identified as a witness to the truth.

2

Thought

(i) THE CHRISTOCENTRIC FOCUS OF KIERKEGAARD'S THEOLOGICAL REFLECTION

The Temptation of Humanism and its Alternative: Socrates and the Teacher

In the *Fragments*, Kierkegaard presents his fundamental problem, both personal and theological—the attractiveness of humanism. The mentors of the *Fragments* and the *Postscript* are Socrates and Lessing, not Christ. The humanism of Socrates is an idealized humanism derived from ancient sources and enriched with insights from the enlightenment and from Hegel. His Socrates is not merely the witty and ironic Athenian, but rather a man of moral and religious sensitivity and encompassing humanity. This restructured Socrates is the temptation.

The point of departure from the Socratic is the existential assertion that the moment is decisive in the sense that men are responsible for what they choose to make of themselves through their choices. Only a major turning such as repentance is able to undo what men have chosen, and such is impossible to man. 'If the moment is decisive' is the only differentiation which Kierkegaard thinks necessary between the Socratic and Christianity. Kierkegaard illustrates the Socratic in terms of the old Platonic notion of recollection to the effect that man is potentially in possession of the truth, is capable of solving his own problems, and of delivering himself from all evils—moral or natural. *This is the fundamental challenge to the Christian faith whether it is expressed through the doctrine of the sufficiency of reason, the sufficiency of science, or an Hegelian faith in historical progress.*

As opposed to the Socratic or humanistic view that man is in possession of sufficient powers, Kierkegaard suggests as an intellectual experiment that man is destitute of the truth, that he is in error. This error is not simply an accident because then it would not be decisive. Man is himself responsible for his error. But if one is responsible for being in error (or as it will later be expressed 'in sin') how does one know it? The logical suggestion is that one in error does not know he is in error. Someone else would have to tell him, and truth here emerges as interpersonal. A new character is added to Kierkegaard's intellectual experiment : the teacher.

Truth also emerges in the Socratic as interpersonal, but it is not such a dire thing to be shut off from the truth. If one does not know the truth one's ignorance is natural because according to the doctrine of recollection man did know the truth previously and forgot it at birth. Education is a remembering. We can demythologize Plato's doctrine of recollection and say that man has the potentiality for knowing, but needs the occasion of a Socrates who does not himself communicate the truth, but rather creates the situation in which the learner can discover the truth for himself.

Truth, in our experiment in thought, is not something which is implicit in man, for man is by his own responsibility in error. The teacher reveals to the man that he is in error and he cannot free himself from it. For if one could free one's self from error the moment would be of no decisive importance. So the teacher is judge. He also restores the condition which enables the learner to appropriate the truth, so he is saviour. The teacher gives the condition by which the disciple's self-imposed state of error can be remedied, so he is also redeemer. And this saving and re-deeming act we could call the atonement. Socrates causes none of these changes in the learner ; it is not merely an ironic state-ment when Socrates says that he can do nothing for the learner.

Turning to the disciple we find that when the teacher gives him the condition he is a new creature. When Socrates and the learner dialectically come to the truth, the best that can be said is that they are better informed. The change in the Socratic is from ignorance to self-discovery. For the disciple and the teacher the change can be called conversion. The change is taking leave from error and can be called repentance. No such change characterizes the Socratic analysis. To receive the condition, to experience a change in the depth of one's being, is a new birth. All this takes place in what we may call the fullness of time, and that moment is decisive. The corresponding Socratic analogy is an accidental occasion.

This brief introduction shows the disjunction Kierkegaard makes between humanism and Christianity. The fundamental distinction between God's sufficiency and human insufficiency, between God's grace and man's cleverness, between God's foolishness and man's wisdom should be made. The most important thing is the fact that the revelation, if we may now use the term, is the teacher himself. The teacher does not reveal certain propositions which would constitute knowledge but rather the teacher who reveals himself is the god. (Throughout, Kierkegaard uses 'the god' to emphasize the hypothetical nature of his discussion.) In the Socratic there is the declaration that no new teaching is delivered because all knowledge is implicit in man and requires only to be made explicit by the dialectic.

The god does not need the disciple as an occasion for his own self-understanding. For the god in so far as he thinks himself would think himself with omniscient clarity. In the Socratic the learner provides the occasion for the teacher to understand himself. According to the new project of thought the learner owes everything to the teacher because he would not otherwise have known that he was in error. In the Socratic the teacher and the learner may arrive at self-understanding as a result of the exchange. Ideally speaking, at the human level no one owes anybody anything, but in the project of thought we are entertaining, the student owes everything to the teacher.

Furthermore, the god is under no necessity to reveal himself. What could possibly move the god to reveal himself? Is it the god's love—not for himself because he is not in need—but for man? Man is in self-imposed error and as a result is separated from the god. In the Socratic, Socrates satisfies the demands of his own being by questioning the student.

Now we are faced with a very difficult problem : How can the god reveal himself? There was once a people who understood that if a man saw God he would die. God is not like man and how can that which is unlike man ever be known by man? It is in this context that Kierkegaard tells one of the most beautiful stories in all his writings.

The king loved the maiden and would have her be queen at his side, but how can the king win the maiden? The first and most obvious thing which would come to mind is that the king should simply show himself in his regal glory and declare his intention. However, this would not do because if the king reveals himself to the maiden she will be overwhelmed and dazzled by his presence. She will give glory to the king but the king does not seek his glory, but hers. We might think that the king would simply elevate her to his side, but she will never be able to overcome the fact that she was a lowly maiden and was simply picked up and clothed in unfamiliar garments and made the object of a strange ceremony. He knows she will never be at home or at ease in such a situation. How then can the king reveal himself? Perhaps we could suggest that he put on the clothes of a peasant and visit her as a lowly man, poor and hungry, but that would not alter the situation—he would still be the king. Up to this point the analogy of the revelation of the god is accurate. If the king will win the maiden he must become a peasant, and there the analogy breaks down because most kings will not become peasants. This is the glory and humility of the god, because he did descend in the form of a servant. The only way that the god can reveal himself is to appear as an humble man among men.

Lapsing permanently into more ordinary theological language one may ask, 'But is this incarnation a revealing or a hiding?' The form of the servant is authentic. He is truly man. If one says that he is also truly God, this stuns the imagination and is a scandal to the reason. There is God. Where is He? There He is being born in a stable, or there He is dying on a cross. That is God? Yes, God so chose to reveal Himself. God's humility is more unimaginable than His glory.

Humanism was for Kierkegaard the major alternative to Christianity. Humanism can be a base and gross form of paganism, but the humanism of which he speaks is an idealized conception. Kierkegaard has proposed as a project of thought that one examine an alternative to humanism, and he differentiates the Christian from the Socratic in a Socratic fashion. The result is that Kierkegaard's reader is dialectically compelled to take one or the other alternative.

The Objective Reality of the Incarnation: The Absolute Paradox

Having vividly demonstrated the dialectical difficulties involved in God's act of self-revelation, Kierkegaard turns to the problem of the apprehension of the objective reality of that revelation. If the king would reveal himself to the maiden, he must renounce his kingship. The god must become a man in order to reveal himself to men. But how can man comprehend God's becoming man? Man cannot comprehend the actuality of the incarnation. If we are to comprehend God's appearance to man as a man, we must know what man is. Socrates, whose self-appointed task was self-knowledge, was not sure whether he was a stranger monster than Typhon or a creature of a simpler sort. It is unlikely that scientific methodologies, not being dedicated to the question regarding human nature, will reveal what man is. If we do not know what man is, how can we presume to know what God's appearing as man would be like? We are up against a paradox : Socrates is a man, but he does not know what man is.

However, let us assume that we know what man is and accept the Socratic view that every individual is 'Man'. A second difficulty arises : How can we know that and what God is? Here again reason is attempting to conceive what cannot be conceived, and to know the unknown. How can unaided reason know God's existence?

Kierkegaard examines the various proofs for God's existence and finds that all of these are misdirected for two fundamental reasons, one logical and one religious. The logical objection to the proofs is that '. . . if the God does not exist it would of course be impossible to prove it ; and if he does exist it would be folly to attempt it'.[2] The religious objection to proofs of God's existence is : If one attempts to prove the existence of God, one only proves what a very wise man he is. Such is Kierkegaard's two-pronged attack against efforts to prove God's existence.

Typical of the philosophers who wish to prove God's existence is St. Thomas Aquinas who wrote :

> The existence of God and other like truths about God which can be known by natural reason are not articles of faith . . . Nevertheless, there is nothing to prevent a man who cannot grasp its proof, accepting, as a matter of faith, something in itself capable of being known and demonstrated.[3]

Kierkegaard argues that faith is the only religiously significant way to know God and that philosophic knowledge is insufficient. This is fundamental to Kierkegaard's attack against Hegel's system, against reflection and against any philosophy—that it would take pride in itself by putting faith in less than a primary position as Aquinas has done in the above quotation. Faith is not something which lacks evidence, nor a psychological condition for the simple-minded and naive, nor for those who have not had the opportunity or talent to earn a Ph.D. in religious philosophy. Faith is the religious dimension simply as such. Though faith will and does seek understanding, it is not founded upon the understanding, but is the existence-orientation of the individual. What faith is might be expressed thus : Faith is commitment to God on a man-to-man basis, because the God we know is the God who was a man.

[2] *Fragments*, (Princeton Univ. Press, 1962), p. 49.
[3] St. Thomas Aquinas, *Summa Theologica*, Part I, Question II, Second Article, Reply Objection I. Cited in Thomas, *Subjectivity and Paradox*, p. 78.

From a philosophical point of view, Kierkegaard has numerous objections against the proofs for God's existence. Primarily, he opposes the ontological argument in Spinoza's form though we can be certain he knew it also in the work of Anselm, Descartes and Hegel. Kierkegaard's argument is complex and condensed, combining something old and something new. His first remark sounds rather like the traditional criticism to the effect that it does not adequately distinguish ideal and factual existence. More significant, however, is Kierkegaard's objection to the concept of the gradation of being which has been such a commonplace of western thought since Plato's *Symposium*. This concept identifies being and perfection in such a way that the more perfection a thing has the more being it has and vice versa. Kierkegaard objects to this principle saying :

> In the case of factual being it is meaningless to speak of more or less of being. A fly, when it is, has as much being as God ; with respect to factual being the stupid remark I here set down has as much being as Spinoza's profundity, for factual being is subject to the dialectic of Hamlet : to be or not to be. Factual being is wholly indifferent to any and all variations in essence, and everything that exists participates without petty jealousy in being, and participates in the same degree. Ideally, to be sure, the case is quite different. *But the moment I speak of being in the ideal sense I no longer speak of being, but of essence.*[4]

This remark puts Kierkegaard in a prominent modern tradition of philosophy which denies grades of perfection and puts all factual existence on a par.

This concern with factual existence separates Kierkegaard and all existentialists from the more metaphysically inclined tradition from Plato to the present and has wide implications. For Hegel, being is also graded, though not ontologically or essentially but rather historically. Hegel's philosophy of history and his *Phenomenology of Mind* show a distinct move from immediate and unreflective systems of consciousness to mediated and reflective systems of consciousness. As spirit or mind progresses historically it is more clearly conscious and more fully developed.

[4] *Fragments*, pp. 51-52.

Kierkegaard's critique of the concept of ontological perfection, the great chain of being or the principle of plentitude, here finds its true resting-place. However, it should be emphasized that though Hegel historicizes the concept of the gradation of being, it is still part of the same tradition. Hegel also uses this tradition to elaborate his own justification of the ontological argument, but Kierkegaard does not explicitly criticize Hegel's argument.

A second critique which Kierkegaard makes of the ontological and causal arguments is that we always reason *from* existence and not *toward* existence. To try to prove Napoleon's existence from his deeds is logically curious. Either we assert that these deeds are Napoleon's from the start or we never derive the existence of Napoleon from them. If we do not assume Napoleon's existence, the best we can do is say that these deeds are the deeds of a military genius. If we stipulate that these kinds of things are the kinds of things that a Napoleon would do, then we can derive Napoleon's existence from them. But then the 'proof' is a *petitio principii*. Kierkegaard's critique of the causal arguments for God's existence is simply that we do not reason *to* existence but rather *from* existence.

The causal arguments for God's existence are also a *petitio principii* because at the very beginning we presuppose an ideal interpretation of existence and will not let anything count against it, even the presence of evil. What is shown is not the existence of God but rather the tenacity of our explanations. The problem boils down to this : in the effects God is not directly or even indirectly given. If we stipulate that only God can produce effects such as these and then name the effects, we have assumed God's existence and have not stated a proof. If we talk about the goodness of nature, the wisdom and the government of the world, these are things which are not at all given in the simple brute data of everyday existence. They represent an ideal interpretation and a most terrible temptation to doubt. How could we go from such an order that we know which is full of absurdity, irrationality, in which chance and accident have such a tremendous role, to an ideal interpretation of governance or providence? These notions, governance and providence, are not given immediately. We can impose this ideal interpretation upon events as we know them and prove that God exists. But we must recognize the fact that we have imposed or presupposed an ideal interpretation and so it all boils down to our old friend, the *petitio principii*, again.

One could reply to this critical exposition that between Napoleon and his deeds there was a contingent relationship, whereas between God and his effects there is what Kierkegaard calls an 'absolute relation'. It is most difficult to grasp what this supposed contingent relation between Napoleon and his deeds would be like. It probably means that someone else could have done them or that it was at one time possible that Napoleon could do otherwise. If someone else did the deeds, there is no possibility that they could help us prove Napoleon's existence which was our actual concern. There would be no contingent relation between them and Napoleon because there would be no relation at all.

The fundamental reason that the notion of an absolute relation is of no help in proving God's existence is that when we begin our proof we presuppose an ideal interpretation of nature which is not itself a part of nature, or, we might add, of historical phenomena. We have been along this path before. Kierkegaard is not willing to present God's existence logically as a proven statement in a metaphysical system, for the simple reason that he cannot find any such proof which carries its own weight.

The previous point regarding the nature of man was that we cannot know what man is. The point at present is that we cannot know even *that* God is. The obvious emerging point regarding the incarnation is : How can we know what the God-man would be like, that he is, or what he is? The incarnation cannot be rationally known.

At this point Kierkegaard introduces a very fundamental notion—the concept of the leap. If we are to know the existence of God, the existence of the God-man, it will have to be by means of a leap. God does not appear to reason, but he appears in

another category—the category of faith, to use a theological
rather than athletic expression. Faith is the subjective reality of
the incarnation.

We cannot know God. We cannot know man. How can we
know the God-man? As pointed out earlier, if God is to reveal
himself in order to redeem man he must become man. But who
is this God and who is this Man? Who is this God-man? In this
breach of reason, reason finds its own glory only in so far as it
knows its limitations. Kierkegaard pointed out the most glorious
glory of reason because he has indicated not just one thing that
reason cannot think : he has pointed out three things. Reason
is brought to a standstill by the paradox of attempting to think
the unthinkable.

There are two possibilities for the absolute paradox, the
paradox of the God-man. One can accept it ; one can reject it.
The happy resolution of the absolute paradox is that a man
receives it in faith with love's understanding for he loves God.
The other alternative is a misunderstood love. Perhaps we
should say misunderstood self-love, for Kierkegaard says man
loves himself inordinately. This reaction to the absolute paradox
is an offence. It is to be overwhelmed by our own inordinate
self-love. So reason is helpless. How can one accept this
absolute paradox?

It can only be believed because it is absurd. A proposition
cannot be the object of both faith and reason at one and the same
time and in one and the same senses. This applies in full measure
to the absolute paradox. As we mentioned in the introduction,
Kierkegaard practised the principle of parsimony to an extensive
degree. He has not made any radical revisions in the traditional
doctrine of God (theology proper) or any revisions in the classical
formation of Christology. In fact, he has simply let orthodoxy
alone. What he has done is to insist that the whole of Christian
theology is finally one point—namely, that Jesus Christ is God-
man.

Furthermore, his practice of the principle of parsimony has
extended to the notion of miracle. Pascal in his *Pensées* offends

reason deeply because he has so many miracles. He not only has the miracles of the church, but also the miracles performed by the devil. For Kierkegaard there is only one absolutely unqualified miracle—namely, the incarnation. Everything else is subservient to this. Kierkegaard would not argue about the other miracles. He is content merely to introduce the category in one case.

Kierkegaard has great wisdom as a Christian apologist because he says there is only one thing of which we need to convince men : this crying baby, this dead man, was and is actually God. Apologetic is the proclamation itself. Apologetic does not exist alongside theology proper and is not an instrument (for use on intellectuals) in the evangelist's toolbox. The three terms, proclamation, apologetic and theology are merely three words for the same activity on the part of the church and have the same conceptual content.

The Relation of History and Faith

If the God-man has appeared, these questions immediately arise : Why now rather than then? Why here rather than there? These questions go to the very heart of the problem surrounding the particularity of the revelation in the incarnation, and the answers given to these will bear effectively upon the relation which this revelation will have to other times and places and to other religions. Kierkegaard does not address himself to all these problems, though one could perhaps extrapolate from his doctrine significant answers to them. What is the relation of faith and history—history being both spatially and temporally conceived ? What is the cognitive relationship between this Christ-event and the observers and those who later hear of it?

Kierkegaard delineates very carefully what is meant by the disciple. Supposing the incarnation is real and this God-man attracts to him a large multitude, but being part of this multitude is not the same as being a disciple. The multitude may come out of curiosity or out of boredom, but neither curiosity nor boredom will qualify one to be a disciple. The disciple is defined by faith. Some may have followed closely and listened carefully, or taken down stenographic reports of the words of the teacher. Their accurate historical knowledge would not pass as faith and one's lack of such information does not indicate unbelief. Perhaps some who are gifted in drawing have followed him and have delineated every line of his face depicting anger, compassion and love. But even such artistic interpretations of his appearance are not faith. To be sure whole multitudes would be historically contemporary with the teacher ; but historical immediacy is not faith.

How does faith come? As we saw earlier, it must be given by God ; therefore it is neither an act of knowledge nor an act of will, but a miracle. The concept of miracle is now used in a purely secondary sense. When one receives happily and lovingly the God-man, it is the miraculous gift of faith. It is miraculous because paradoxically, faith could not be an object of knowledge nor could it be an act of will since the condition for it must be given. It is the act of God.

The contemporary disciple receives thereby no advantage from hearing the words or seeing the face because faith is defined as the conditions given by God and not by historical accidents.

A further question occurs immediately : What about those who are not contemporary? What about those who live later, who never see the teacher, but only hear reports of him? If one skips several hundred years—Kierkegaard happily considers skipping 1,843 years—and comes to the last generation, one finds that they are temporally removed from the shock of the event. However, this does not mean they suffer a disadvantage since the condition is given by one who is always present.

If anything, the last generation may find itself embarrassed by historical accumulations ; after all, the faith has now been around for nineteen centuries and the necessity for faith may be less obvious due to the sheer weight of accumulated testimonials. But just as the sound of the teacher's voice and the expression on his face did not substitute for faith, so now, the accumulated evidence of a couple of millennia of belief and faith will not substitute for the condition which only God can give.

Christianity, the Christ-event, or faith in the Christ-event is transcendent and can be believed only because of the condition given by God. And so all men stand equal—those who saw the face and heard the words as well as those who lived several years later and who did not see the face or hear the words. There is neither advantage nor disadvantage in being contemporary with the event or living two millennia or a hundred millennia after the event. Faith is always a supernatural occurrence and the condition is given by God.

To return to the questions with which the section opened : Why now rather than then? Why here rather than there? We find a very simple answer. There is no difference, because the condition given by God who is eternally present is equally available to all regardless of spatial or temporal differences.

Philosophical Implications of Revelation

The major problem posed by the foregoing exposition is the analysis of motion and change. The questions are, 'What happens when something comes into existence? Assuming that it is the same plan or essence which is before possible and after actual, what happens when something moves from possibility to actuality?' Kierkegaard's reply is that everything that comes into existence does so by an act of freedom.

The coming into being which concerns Kierkegaard is not physical change but historical change. The historical, being empirical and factual, is subject to the whole set of considerations which imply that our statements about the empirical are at best probable statements because the empirical is the realm of contingency. However, we find in the history of philosophy that this position is contested by many people of high authority, including Hegel.

Hegel in his philosophy tried to unite being and thought and to write a philosophy in which the whole description of man's historical existence would have dialectical necessity. For Hegel, the concept of possibility is virtually non-existent. The term occurs in his logic, but it is dialectically changed into necessity. Such a view was maintained by some ancient writers as well as some more recent.

As Bertrand Russell expressed it in *Mysticism and Logic*, 'We all regard the past as determined simply by the fact that it has happened ; but for the accident that memory works backward and not forward, we should regard the future as equally determined by the fact that it will happen.'[5] It is just this identification of the necessity of the past (because it cannot be changed) with the possibility of the future to which Kierkegaard objects. To be sure the past as past cannot be changed, but this specific unchangeableness does not mean that it was necessary before it became past. There was a time when that which is now past was possible and Kierkegaard argues that along with that which became actual there were several other possibilities, any of which could have occurred. Only one possibility happens, but when it passes from possibility to actuality and then lapses into the past it does not thereby become necessary. If it were necessary now that it is, as Hegel and Russell maintained, it would have been necessary also when it was in the future. But this is simply to make an illusion of freedom. Kierkegaard denies this interpretation and maintains that freedom is real and that the past when it was still future was open just as we now consider the future to be open. Kierkegaard has performed a valuable conceptual analysis of 'necessity' in relation to history.

The theological significance of this point is that according to Hegel's philosophy, the Christ-event had to occur and that even God is not free of dialectical necessity. Hegel's philosophy eliminates the miracle, in the first sense and in the second sense. Hegel rejects the miracle in the first sense because he rejects the

5 Cited, *Fragments*, n., p. 239-40.

possibility of the incarnation as the free act of God's self-revelation, saying that it was necessary and subordinate to the dialectical self-movement of the absolute. He also rejects miracle in the second sense but not by reference to the notion of necessity. For Hegel, faith is immediacy and is a dialectically undeveloped aspect of consciousness. It is the task of philosophy to bring man from faith to reason. Believing in the incarnation then is not a gift of grace, but is rather undeveloped philosophical insight which requires philosophy to explain it. Faith is eliminated in favour of knowledge. Faith as contingent upon God's gift and the human reception of God's gift loses its traditional theological sense in Hegel.

The principal theological import of Kierkegaard's discussion of possibility and necessity is that the historical is merely a matter of belief and it can be understood only as such. This is apparent when one attempts to establish an historical event, particularly one for which the historical evidence is slight. A well-documented recent historical event is not quite so obviously a matter of belief, but it is, as the conflicting testimony about the assassination of President Kennedy shows. If this is true of ordinary historical events, what about the Christ-event, this breaking of the eternal into the temporal? It cannot be merely an object of ordinary belief, but an object of faith in an extraordinary and unusual sense. Here the actual historical content is difficult to establish because something transhistorical is claimed to be present in this unique event. Such an unusual occurrence cannot be grasped by reason at all. It can only be grasped if one goes beyond reason to another category—to faith.

At a number of points Kierkegaard's argument seems to be approaching certain classical positions regarding the scope and means of knowledge. He also offers some remarkable innovations. For instance, his criticisms of the efforts to prove God's existence are a combination of strict adherence to logical principles and genuine religious fervour unique in the history of philosophy. His general approach to epistemological problems puts him with those whom William James called the 'tough-

c

minded', but his preference for empiricism is not narrow or restricted by some *a priori* consideration concerning what can be experienced. Unfortunately, empiricism, by giving first priority to clarity and simplicity, has yielded to the temptation to prescribe limits for itself and thereby to exclude from consideration any instances of experience which would compromise its first priorities. In so doing, empiricism has become hard and narrow, excluding the really vital concerns of the living human being. For Kierkegaard, on the other hand, any report of experience at all becomes grist for his mill. He rejects the typical empirical priorities for inclusiveness and existential concern. The objective of philosophical and theological analysis is descriptive, not prescriptive. Empiricism is for Kierkegaard radical and goes to the root of any human experience. The sense of guilt as a human experience is as philosophically meaningful for Kierkegaard as the analysis of cause would be for Hume. Hume would probably dogmatically exclude guilt because it is neither a statement regarding a matter of fact nor a relation of ideas. Kierkegaard would probably say of Hume's candidate that it is speculatively interesting but probably not too existentially meaningful. Yet, Kierkegaard does in fact have more to say about 'cause' than Hume about 'guilt', and so is the more inclusive and catholic philosopher.

It is precisely this concern with the broadly human which provides the anthropocentric antithesis to the theocentric focus of his work.

(ii) THE ANTHROPOCENTRIC FOCUS OF KIERKEGAARD'S THEOLOGICAL REFLECTION

This section relates to themes Kierkegaard considered 'psychological' although the term may be misleading today. A number of words will be used to attempt to achieve clarity, including his own 'psychology'.

The psychological themes are illuminated in two works. The

first is *The Concept of Dread*, which was published only four days after *The Philosophical Fragments*, and the second is *Sickness Unto Death*. In them Kierkegaard attempts a complete rethinking of the nature of sin and the human psyche. Difficulty is added because the attempt is made within the context of a long and extended critique upon Hegel and the German romantics.

When we referred to the story of the king and the maiden, we were dealing only with the perplexity faced by the king in revealing himself to the maiden. It is also necessary to deal with the maiden's problem of whether or not to accept the king's love. We may have assumed that everything was well with the maiden, but Kierkegaard rejected this assumption, as must all Christian theology. Revelation is further complicated because God is not necessarily revealing himself to one who will receive the revelation with openness, freedom and love. Strange as it may seem, man thinks of God as his enemy. Why is man alienated from God? What is the ontological condition of man which God would remedy in the incarnation?

Man's condition is complex because his internal constitution is both finite and infinite. This is no mere 'unregenerate Hegelianism' but is the key to the understanding of man in his spiritual dimension. Finite, in a state of self-development, dying, he nevertheless grasps after the infinite, the eternal, the ideal, the boundless. The more clearly man can conceive of this otherness which he is not but would be, the deeper is his sense of alienation. Resentful of this limitation (and possibly others) he despairs and rebels, for he cannot 'be like the most high'. Ideally man is a possible harmony of finitude and infinitude, but if the harmony does not occur or is ruptured, the self's reintegration is possible only through grace or a divine recreation. Kierkegaard conceived of man as *intended* for this integration of finitude and infinitude.

The ego *is not*, but is rather in a state of becoming which is directed by choice, and so alienation in all its forms, or sin, is a result of choice. Therefore, one might possibly think that sin is a proper object of discussion within the sphere of ethics.

Kierkegaard thinks rather that ethics holds up the ideality of moral obligation. Sin sometimes, indeed frequently, involves a repudiation of the ethical, but it is not defined within the ethical. Ethics is a secular or philosophic category saying what man should be ; sin is a theological category clarifying what man unfortunately is. Upon the concept of sin ethics founders ; although ethics can command, it can give neither the power to perform the command nor the power to forgive moral failure.

In the Beginning—Adam

The analysis of the psychological origins of sin begins with Adam, who must not be given a special position. Kierkegaard begins with Adam because of his deep commitment to the idea of the solidarity of the race. Adam as an individual is essentially the race, and the race is essentially Adam in any meaningful explanation of original sin. Therefore, whatever will explain Adam and his fall into sin will explain sinfulness of the race and whatever will explain the continuity of sin in the race will explain Adam's sin.

Adam is responsible for the 'first sin' which is not like any other sin because it is *the* sin and it established a new quality in existence. There is a difference between the first sin of any individual and the first sin of Adam in the sense that sinfulness does not enter the world by means of the first sin of every man, but it occurs in the same way in any individual as it occurred first in Adam. Thus Adam is not outside the race. The sinfulness of the race goes right on and on, adding sin to sin in a quantitative way, whereas the individual when he first sins comes to participate in sin by means of a 'leap into the quality' of sinfulness.

Before man sins, he is innocent. Innocence is a quality of personality which every man loses essentially as did Adam—namely by guilt, which is what makes Adam's sin like ours and ours like his, and renders the account in Genesis the only consistent one. Innocence could have continued. It is only lost by means of a leap, a qualitative change, a decision to sin which is chosen by the individual.

The only possible explanation of the leap into original sin then must be in innocence itself. Kierkegaard accepts a rather romantic notion of innocence as a state of being at peace and in harmony with oneself and one's environment. The innocent soul becomes self-consciously aware of the potentiality that it can become almost anything. In the face of this unknown the ego falls into anxiety or dread. Fear has an object, but anxiety is before nothing, and has no object. The innocent experiences dread when faced by that which it neither loves nor desires, but yet chooses.

Anxiety is the reality of freedom, a freedom to become anything or nothing. Anxiety is the confrontation with possibility simply as such ; undefined, unqualified, indefinite. The transition from innocence (and anxiety) to guilt takes place by means of the leap. When one begins the leap, one is innocent ; when the leap is finished, one is guilty. The leap, the choice of sin itself, is beyond theological or psychological explanation. It is not that one desires the sin and consequent guilt ; therefore concupiscence is not fundamental. It is not that one loves guilt, but before infinite possibility or before nothing the soul sinks from weakness and lapses into anxiety which is itself guiltless. One does not even know whether what he can choose is good or evil ; but he knows that he can. The choice is made and the soul is guilty because the choice is in the direction of egoism, not faith.

As a result of sin, guilt appears which transforms sensuousness (according to Genesis) into sexuality by shame. The problem of sexuality and sensuousness is very complex, and Kierkegaard throughout all his works insisted that sensuousness is not the same as sexuality. In the state of sin, sensuousness is transformed into sexuality which is then the source of generations and of history. It might appear that Kierkegaard argues that the fall is fortunate, but he is not doing so. The fall could be conceived as fortunate only if we insist that the primal condition of innocence was less than what God wanted for man. The primal state

D

of innocence of which we now have only mythological hints—
both toward the past and toward the future, toward Eden and
toward Heaven—is what God wanted of man and is man's best
estate. In fallen man, sexuality is the opposition to spirit and is
the mark of his fallenness. This mark will remain until innocence
is restored. With innocence restored, there will still be sensuousness (the resurrected body) but not sexuality.

This argument concerning anxiety and the fall may furthermore seem to indicate that the fall was necessary. Nothing could
be further from the truth. In fact, Kierkegaard is quite adamant
and sarcastic to anyone who would ask the question, 'What if
Adam had not sinned?' However, this is not quite so foolish as
he seems to suggest. Kierkegaard raises the possibility that there
could have been an original qualitative leap—not from innocence
to sin, but rather from innocence to faith. This was a possibility,
but the one which freedom did not attain. The realization that
freedom can and does put one in anxiety, however, does not
mean that dread and the resultant guilt are necessary. Man
chooses in such a way that guilt rather than faith results and it is
his responsibility. Formerly this fundamental choice of egocen-
tricity was called pride, but perhaps it should be called sloth. It
is not that man in guilt and the resultant sin is *more* than God
wanted him to be. This Faustian and Promethean interpretation
of sin is incorrect. It is rather that in guilt and the resultant sin
man is less than God intended him to be. The original sin is not
pride but sloth or laziness.

The marvellous 'I can' is impotent. One simply swoons in
dizziness and impotence. Freedom is too strenuous for man,
and so from lassitude he chooses to be less than man. This
reversal of interpretation from pride to laziness and impotence
is of no small significance because it robs the original fall of our
natural approval of the rebel.

Sometimes Kierkegaard has been accused of saying that
'original sin' was not a sin. This is patently silly, for an original
sin is by definition an original sin. However, original sin is not
so much Kierkegaard's concern as is its presupposition. Prior

to, and hence more 'original' or primitive than the original sin, is innocence and its consequent anxiety, and the burden of freedom.

Kierkegaard's position is difficult because he is labouring to do two things. He is making a supreme effort to remain within the orthodox reformed tradition which maintained that after Adam an individual was no longer able to avoid evil. He is also attempting to maintain that each individual before he individually sins is innocent, and that when he does sin he is responsible for his own sin. Thus also Kierkegaard attempts to defend his position against the charge of Pelagianism while maintaining the reality of sin and complete personal responsibility. In this contest between the inheritance of original sin and the original innocence and consequent responsibility of every individual for his own sin, Kierkegaard has his finger on one of the really severe problems of Christian theology.

Kierkegaard has presented an interpretation which he hopes will satisfy both of these requirements. He has maintained the solidarity of the race through posterity so that in Adam all are lost. Sin accumulates quantitatively in history so that history is indeed the history of sin. Though all men have sinned, their sin was not necessary because of the sin of Adam, inheritance or any such construction of thought. Each man sins because he himself chooses to sin ; he is originally innocent—as innocent as Adam ; his choice is just as free as Adam's, his anxiety just as original, his responsibility just as complete.

From Anxiety to the Forms of Despair

Yet, when one does sin, this is not the end of the anxiety for it continues to accumulate and is transformed in the world through sin. Men enter into new forms of dread. Kierkegaard discusses the dread of evil or remorse which is directed not only to the past but also to the future. One has remorse, not only with reference to the sins one has committed but also to the sins which one may commit. One recognizes that one will sin because one has sinned. The only thing which could possibly destroy remorse is faith, which Kierkegaard defines as courage. It requires courage to renounce anxiety without anxiety, but such is not within the power of man ; it is only within the power of God.

Besides such anxiety with regard to evil, there is another category—the demonic, or the anxiety with regard to the good. In the dread of the good, the soul, now in sin, dreads the possibility of salvation or redemption, and the soul sinks deeper into anxiety and denies its own possibility. It feels that it is evil, is bound to evil and cannot respond to grace, redemption, or to mercy. So the demonical shuts itself up refusing to look upon revelation and to accept grace. In this shut-up condition, despair is intensified into a more decisive and complete bondage to sin, and this second bondage is more decisive than the first. The theological dimension of sin is now complete.

The structures which we have examined to this point concern themselves largely with anxiety. Dread is at this point transmuted into despair. The dizziness of freedom which results in dread is recognized as being different from the despair which one feels after sin. One is guilty after the choice made in the dizziness of freedom because such choices reflect egoism rather than faith. This anxiety is raised to a new level of intensity in despair because despair is the rejection of grace and mercy ; whereas original guilt was the rejection of innocence. This conception of anxiety or dread relates to the myth of Adam and the dogmatic problem of original sin ; despair relates to the structures of man's continued isolation and rejection of grace and mercy. Thus the dread of the good is despair or the 'sickness unto death'.

Pushing his argument deeper and deeper into subjectivity, Kierkegaard characterizes the self in a fashion which shows the possibility of despair. Since man is spirit which manifests itself in a relation of body and soul (as we learned previously), all sorts of misrelationships are possible. If one wills in despair to be oneself or not to be oneself, or if one is not even conscious of having a self, then one has violated the fundamental constitution of one's own being and broken a relationship with the power which established it. The only possibility for the condition of health within a self is for the self to relate itself to itself, and this is possible only by being in relation to the power which has established it. Authentic selfhood is possible only in a faithful relation to God.

Kierkegaard states two possible misrelations. The possibility of defiant self-assertiveness in which one attempts to be more than oneself, or the possibility of underdevelopment in which one decides to be less than oneself, represents the sickness unto death—despair. Kierkegaard stated in *The Concept of Dread* that the fall is the result of dizziness or is indicative of impotent egoism. In his consideration of despair, he recognizes the possibility of the overdevelopment of the self. One can despairingly will to be oneself and this is defiance. Whereas anxiety is impotence, despair can be either weakness or defiance. The only way that these may be overcome is through a proper relationship to the divine through faith.

The nature of man is also a possible unity of finitude and infinitude, and this dialectical tension allows two possibilities. Despair can be the despair of infinitude which is 'the lack of finitude'. The person recognizes no limits to himself and to what he himself could be. He immerses and bathes himself in fantasy and in imagination. He attempts imaginatively to indulge every possibility which his will suggests.

Another form of despair is the despair of finitude, or a lack of infinitude, or a lack of spirit or vision. The person who lacks infinity turns out to be the organization man as we recognize him today. In this first and most suggestive analysis, Kierkegaard strikes many of the themes which are struck by later existentialists in their descriptions of inauthentic existence. The person who lacks infinity is the one who is simply ground smooth as a pebble or as a well-used coin. This is the man who finds no embarrassments in life. Though he may have to work at it, he finds life easy and comfortable and he gets on in all his worldly affairs. He manages to succeed in the face of dishonesty by being dishonest, in the face of violence by being violent, and in the face of mediocrity by being mediocre. The one who lacks infinity becomes a sheep or only a parody of a man. He is a man who lacks audacity, honesty, courage, integrity—manhood itself.

Kierkegaard enunciates his position not only with regard to the various forms of despair but also with regard to the possibility of offence. It is one thing to say that man is in sin ; it is another thing to say that it is possible for a man to be free from sin. In the defiant form of despair one sees that despair has led to offence, and yet this is the very thing which must be avoided if one is to accept the paradox of the incarnation.

From Exposition to Existence and to Grace

The exposition of the essential structure of salvation through the God-man, the nature of the fall and of sin, requires for completion an existential description of the encounter of grace by man. Kierkegaard has a very high conception of the church, but for him the church is not the mediator of grace. Grace is rather mediated through Jesus Christ and through the Spirit. It is not possible for the church or any other instrument to mediate between God and man. Here Kierkegaard is closest to the reformed tradition. Strange as it may seem, he is perhaps even closer to the Anabaptist position at this point than he is to that of his own tradition ; because, for the Anabaptist tradition, the church is the community of grace but God's initial saving work takes place outside the church ; and then, after salvation, men become part of the church. Now if the church is not the mediator of grace, how then does the individual come to experience God's grace? To answer this question we must elucidate briefly a summary of the stages on life's way, because grace is met in the very midst of life and history.

Life as it is actually lived in the historical world is lived in three fashions or styles ; or, as Kierkegaard calls them, 'stages'.

They are the aesthetic, the ethical, and the religious. The last is divided into Religion A and Religion B.

The aesthete, characterized in the first volume of *Either/Or* and in the first essay in *Stages on Life's Way*, is aware that he has no ego in the sense that his self is immediate and for the moment. He has avoided making decisions in life and therefore has never become truly a self. He knows too that if he is to become a self he must make certain commitments in life, but he cannot since he prefers to live continuously in the immediate, accepting no moral obligations so that nothing can ever tie him down or hamper his style. But the end of it all is nothingness, nihilism.

This ideal description is existentially impossible because it is all too abstract. No one could live without some ethical commitments, but Kierkegaard has shown how undiluted romanticism and hedonism would appear. Furthermore, this abstract description leading as it does to nihilism, boredom and despair opens up the possibility of another way of life by choosing ethical responsibility instead of nihilism, purpose instead of boredom, and hope of fulfilment instead of despair. The choosing is a leap and, as we have come to expect, it is itself unfathomable.

Judge William, Kierkegaard's moral hero, is the pseudonymous author of the second volume of *Either/Or* and the long essay, 'Observations about Marriage' in the *Stages on Life's Way*. Judge William's view of marriage is a dialectical unity of romanticism and the bourgeois spirit and morality manifest in Hegel. Due to the contemporary impact of the German romantic movement, Kierkegaard's analysis of marriage carries the whole weight of his moral philosophy. If the argument for marriage fails, so does his whole concept of morality.

The immediate object of criticism in his moral philosophy is the rather novel view of marriage and sex which he read in Schlegel's *Lucinde*. Kierkegaard, like Hegel, recognized that, although it was ostensibly an attack upon marriage because marriage was the basic social institution, he saw it also as an attack upon all morality. For Kierkegaard marriage, the ethical, is not hell as the romantics thought, but it is heaven. Marriage was not a joyless concern for the family capital or for the education of the children or for the pettinesses of convenience, as Hegel seemed to think. Kierkegaard says both yes and no to Hegel and to the romantics. He shows how ethics overcomes romantic nihilism and despair (by commitment) and middle-class triviality (by romance).

With Judge William we first come into existential relation with 'Christianity'. Marriage, characterized by commitment and romance, is an ethical relationship between persons, and bears within it the beauty and immediate exhilaration of romanticism, and the moral responsibility of bourgeois views which make it identical with Christian marriage. Judge William unites the aesthetic, the ethical and the religious specifically in marriage. However, religion as described by Judge William is not thoroughly and completely Christian, for he does not mention or show any comprehension of the more dialectical and paradoxical aspects of the Christian religion. Philosophically Judge William's religion is a religion of immanence, and socially it is a 'folk religion' which in his particular case is Christianity.

Though choice or ethical commitment through marriage is central to Judge William's thought, it would be preposterous to think that Kierkegaard made choice such a central thing that it made no difference what choice was made, so long as one earnestly chose. Yet for all Kierkegaard's insistence upon the priority of authentic, personal choice, his insistence occurs within the context of a discussion of the ethical considered as universal. Choice is fundamentally an ethical and religious category for Kierkegaard. What one chooses is important, but it is more important that one choose with the whole pathos of one's being. The content of the choice is of secondary importance, but this means neither that Kierkegaard rejects eternal verities nor that he does not trust in reason. Kierkegaard recognizes the difference between informed and uninformed, reasoned and unreasoned, responsible and irresponsible decisions.

Kierkegaard's insistence upon the centrality of choice in his moral philosophy comes to focus nowhere so radically as it does in the book, *Fear and Trembling*, where ethics is understood as the universal in a purely Kantian or Hegelian sense. If there is to be any bracketing or suspension of the ethical, it can only be under a higher command, and that higher command can only be from God. Some scholars have thought that a higher command from the state or from some political demagogue would suffice in Kierkegaard's eyes. Such is not the case. Kierkegaard elaborated the careful dialectic of *Fear and Trembling* in order to exclude totalitarianism, the state, a political demagogue or a political party as being able to command obligatory behaviour which would be contrary to the ethical.

In ethical choice one finds sufficient opportunity to exercise all the strength and courage of one's personality. One does not have to live very long before one realizes that the ethical commands that which one cannot or does not perform. The ethical is the ideal, but in the actual world we rarely attain our ideals. As a result, we suffer a form of the despair of finitude. Kierkegaard widens the ethical to include the moral precepts of the gospel so that these add to the ethical ideals which bring the idealist closer to an utter despair where there will be a recognition of the need for grace. This 'recognition' is the transition from the ethical stage to the first religious stage, or Religion A.

Religion A for Kierkegaard has for its mentors Socrates and Lessing. Socrates, as pointed out at the beginning, is the epitome of the best of humanity and humanism. In the *Postscript*, Kierkegaard further elaborates his development of Socrates to show that he comes all the way to the border of Christian subjectivity but he does not come into Christian subjectivity. The same is true for Lessing, and perhaps these two coalesce in Kierkegaard's thinking because for both Socrates and Lessing the principal task is to become subjective because subjectivity is truth.

The fundamental concept of Religion A is the statement : *Subjectivity is truth*. This is the most difficult expression in Kierkegaard's philosophy and it is within the limits of supposition that everything that is incorrect that can be said about it

E

has been said by someone. The fundamental text for his doctrine of radical subjectivity is,

> *When the question of truth is raised in an objective manner, reflection is directed objectively to the truth, as an object to which the knower is related. Reflection is not focused upon the relationship, however, but upon the question of whether it is the truth to which the knower is related. If only the object to which he is related is the truth, the subject is accounted to be in the truth. When the question of the truth is raised subjectively, reflection is directed subjectively to the nature of the individual's relationship ; if only the mode of this relationship is in the truth, the individual is in the truth even if he should happen to be thus related to what is not true.*[6]

In this passage Kierkegaard does not obliterate the distinction between truth and falsehood, rather he re-interprets it by insisting that one can be subjectively in untruth as well as in the truth. One's commitment to X does not make X true. If X is untrue, then it is untrue whether or not one is committed to it ; that is, the truth or falsity of X is determined objectively without reference to one's subjective commitment or lack thereof.

It is obvious that men are committed to all sorts of false notions. Kierkegaard is emphasizing that men are not committed to them because they are false, but because they think they are true. The argument is analagous to that in ancient philosophy that all men by nature seek the good. They may in fact seek an evil thing, but they do not seek it because they think it is evil, but rather because they misunderstand it and think it is good. So here men do not commit themselves to something because they think that it is untrue, but rather because they think it is true. If the object of their commitment is false, no amount of commitment will ever change its epistemological character. The issue which he raises is not strictly a matter of knowledge except in so far as his views contradict and criticize the theory of knowledge and methodology of Hegelian idealism. Kierkegaard's views of knowledge are in the direction of empirical realism, but he did not develop a thoroughgoing theory of knowledge and the expression, *truth is subjectivity*, is not intended to express an epistemology in the regular meaning of that term.

Kierkegaard's contribution here is unparalleled in the history of philosophy for he is not especially concerned with knowing the truth but rather with being in the truth or doing the truth. The last expression, *doing the truth*, was no doubt suggested to Kierkegaard from the New Testament : 'But he who does what is true comes to the light, that it may be clearly seen that his deeds have been wrought in God.' (John 3 : 21, RSV.) Kierkegaard does not use that expression in the exposition of his slogan for he is writing in terms which are not drawn from the Bible. To use this term here would be to cross into the realm of Religion B. Here he simply intends to show that there is another dimension to the problem of truth besides that one which is usually the concern of epistemology. Truth is to be acted upon, and sheer speculation about the truth is useless if, and only if, it becomes a substitute for acting on the truth.

This expression, *to do the truth*, or *to act on the truth*, affirms truth in a more fundamentally personal way than epistemological conceptions usually do. To act according to the truth may mean only that one does not walk out of windows on the twentieth floor with the expectation of crossing the street to the building on the other side. Such an acting on the truth is trivial, common and everyday, because it is public knowledge and is not what Kierkegaard has in mind. Not to act on the truth of the law of gravity would be madness. The expression *to act on the truth* has a philosophic importance for Kierkegaard only in cases where the truth acted upon is not public but is rather objectively uncertain. If the truth is subjective (i.e., private) and one still acts on it, then it will be more difficult to explain, but it still may not have the dimensions Kierkegaard claims. For instance, subjective truth at one level is a mere matter of taste. I may say Elvis Presley is a better musician than Bach. What here parades as an objective statement of fact is only a subjective preference. I may act on this subjective preference and buy all of Presley's records. Obviously Kierkegaard does not intend his slogan to serve aesthetics.

An example of subjectivity that is not a matter of taste but rather is a difficult philosophical problem is the knowledge of God. Nothing can demonstratively prove whether God does or does not exist. In the example above, we did have something objective which can be kept in the centre of the discussion : the manuscripts or records of the music. We might give certain criteria about music so as to judge whether a certain musician qualified as a good or bad musician, but whether good or bad, Bach or Presley would have to be called musicians, even by those who might happen to dislike them both. The problem of the existence of God is that there are simply no empirical criteria by which one can make more or less probable his existence or nature. (See above, Part I.) This way of expressing the problem is the objective way, but the subjective way asks whether or not one is related to an object in such a manner that it could be a God relationship.

The subjective way of approaching the question of the knowledge of God is not to ask whether or not God exists or whether this object is indeed the true God, but rather to inquire into the relationship one has to this object. It is not possible to name the criteria by which one can say whether it is the true God or not to which one is related. Truth here means, '*An objective uncertainty held fast in an appropriation-process of the most passionate inwardness is the truth*, the highest truth attainable for an *existing* individual.'[7]

The person who does obtain this most passionate inwardness is Socrates. Yet we have not moved from the understanding of Socrates as ironic and as ignorant, because he is passionately devoted to the truth, whatever truth might be. There is only one way to get beyond the conception of truth as subjectivity ; that one way is to admit that subjectivity is untruth. Subjectivity as developed in the *Postscript* does not come to the full dimension of Christian faith. This exposition demonstrates the deep Socratic humanism of Kierkegaard which, as we pointed out, was for him always the fundamental temptation and would suffice

[7] *Postscript*, p. 182.

to give him the accolade of humanists if he had not written anything except the *Postscript*.

However, Kierkegaard did not think humanism sufficient, and the Socratic form of subjectivity must experience a metamorphosis before it becomes Christian subjectivity. The change is not a change of mediation or even of degree. Christian subjectivity is not an intensification of humanist subjectivity, but it is something new. As Kierkegaard expressed it in the *Fragments*,

> The projected hypothesis indisputably makes an advance upon Socrates, which is apparent at every point. Whether it is therefore more true than the Socratic doctrine is an entirely different question, which cannot be decided in the same breath, since we have here assumed a new organ : Faith ; a new presupposition : the consciousness of Sin ; a new decision : the Moment ; and a new Teacher : the God in Time.[8]

The passage from one of the stages to another could until now be conceived as a dialectical movement of the freely choosing individual. However, at this point, it is not that. The movement to the Christian sphere is neither dialectically nor humanly possible. The aesthetic individual chooses an ethical existence, for he finds that he cannot always be a spectator, that *yes* and *no* and that *good* and *evil* are mutually exclusive possibilities. The ethical individual chooses the religious because of the ambiguity of existence and his own moral failure. The ethical stage for the aesthete and Religion A for the ethical become antithetical possibilities because of the progressive dialectical development of their own existences. But they are dialectical possibilities, not necessities as Hegel would have us believe, because possibility is higher than necessity. It is the act of existing itself that compels a person to choose, yet the movement is willed and the person could suspend action and remain an aesthete or could will to come to terms with the world or with himself and experience a despair of the lack of infinitude. The ethical person could relapse into the position of the aesthete and experience a despair of the lack of finitude.

[8] *Fragments*, p. 139.

Such a choice to suspend action is humanly possible. It is precisely this relation of the person to the world and of the person to himself that reflects the very basis of human existence. Existential relatedness is the one thing overlooked by most speculative and modern philosophy. However, the more subjectively developed the individual is, the more he will realize his own lack of objective certainty in the face of his subjective interests. Subjectivity is not a motto to be flaunted around as if it could guarantee anything. Subjectivity cannot guarantee any truth whatsoever except the integrity and honesty of the human subject in his commitment. If there is to be religious truth it is not from the subject. If there is to be salvation, it cannot originate in the subject who recognizes his own moral failure and need of grace. If there is to be salvation, if there is to be faith, it must be the gift of God. If sin is to be overcome, it must be forgiven by God. And so finally we come to Kierkegaard's central point again, that the whole drama of man terminates in the revelation of God incarnate.

Kierkegaard's final word is not that subjectivity is truth, but rather that subjectivity is untruth. Religion A as we have described it can exist within paganism and even within Christendom for it characterizes every man who is decisively religious but is not decisively Christian. It is quite proper that one should be a full and complete human, that one should be subjectively developed ; but to this point there is no paradox, there is no scandal, there is no faith. Anyone who is to become a Christian, and Kierkegaard's effort was not to make it difficult but only to make it clear, must endure the scandal of the incarnation, the stumbling-block of the cross, the crucifixion of his reason by faith. All of the intricate elaboration of the dialectic of the incarnation, the psychological interpretation of dread as it lapses over into despair, the categories of ordinary human existence come to focus in Kierkegaard's effort not to explain the faith, not to make it rational but to explain why Christianity (Religion B) requires a 'leap' to faith.

3

Significance

ONE of the most important contributions which Kierkegaard has made to contemporary theology is that he has called the church back to the task of theology. After Kierkegaard, theology in the strictest sense is recognized as being the vital life-blood of the church in a way that it had not been for some time, particularly in the eighteenth century. Theology is not something the church may or may not do ; but theology is the fundamental activity of the church and this activity is manifest in evangelism, missions and apologetic.

Kierkegaard has insisted that theology must be done on its own terms, with its own categories and with its own sustained methodology. Theology must neither be formed nor receive its content from philosophical positions alien to its own nature. It is not the business of theology to become intellectually respectable to any time ; because when properly understood, theology will be a scandal and a stumbling-block to the philosophy, the rationalism and the idolatry of any age. No longer must theology cut itself to the size and shape allowed by an Aristotle, a Hegel, or a Kant ; it need not try to incorporate positivism or a social gospel founded upon a notion of social progress. In this sense, Kierkegaard, having penetrated the smoke and haze of the accommodating and intimidated theologies of the eighteenth and early nineteenth centuries, emerges as the first post-modern theologian.

Theology must be theocentric and so it cannot have its point of departure in man, human feelings, human history, or any kind of social ideology. Theology stands in no need of justification from any of these categories, respectable as they are in their own right.

An example of a specific theological disorientation which Kierkegaard overcame is the antithetical view of God's transcendence and immanence expressed in eighteenth and early nineteenth centuries respectively. Frequently the terms, immanence and transcendence, were thought of as contradictory. Philosophy in the early nineteenth century, in reaction to the transcendent God of deism, emphasized in antithesis a God who was immanent in the human heart, in human history and in nature. This immanent God became so closely identified with human history in Hegel's philosophy that ultimately one has only history, and God (as over against or different from history) simply disappears. The death of God, or the substitution of history for God, is not a discovery of recent American theologians but is the meaning of Hegel's philosophy. The immanence of God is also found in the theology of Schleiermacher who, though not an out-and-out pantheist, still fails to appreciate that thrust of the Hebraic tradition which emphasizes the difference between God and man.

These references to Hegel and to Schleiermacher will be sufficient to indicate a trend of nineteenth century theological thought against which Kierkegaard struggled and which we may hope he decisively refuted. It is important to notice that Kierkegaard moves beyond both the nineteenth century compromise and the enlightenment in his concept of the transcendence of God. The otherness of God is not deistic in Kierkegaard but is Hebraic in orientation and content. On the other hand, the immanence of God in Kierkegaard is not romantic in the sense of Schleiermacher nor in the historical sense of Hegel. Rather Kierkegaard's sense of the immanence of God is Hebraic and Christian. Kierkegaard reaches behind the distortions of God's transcendence and immanence in the eighteenth and nineteenth centuries to the reformers and to the biblical sources themselves. His insights represent a recovery of biblical theology, although the recovery is not expounded as biblical theology but as an attempt to recover the existential foundations of Christian theology. For Kierkegaard the point of departure in theology is divine revelation, not a reading, be it ever so accurate, of the human heart or human history.

A principle of economy has several times been mentioned. A specific application perhaps now is in order. Kierkegaard has practised this principle to such an extent that he has finally reduced the Christian faith to a single assertion : in Jesus Christ, God has acted. He has presented this with a minimum of philosophical or theological systematic argumentation, and yet his analysis of the significance and meaning of the fundamental nature of the concept of revelation is overwhelming in its simplicity and subtlety by reducing the problem of the historical Jesus to an insignificant place. If we had only the information contained in a newspaper notice, that a man lived among us who claimed to be God and that he has since died, this information would be more than enough to initiate the dialectical considerations of the possibility of the incarnation. This reduction of the required historical information to virtually zero is most significant in the controversy regarding the Christ of faith versus the Jesus of history. For Kierkegaard, the Christ of faith is sufficient for any and all theological purposes. Edifying purposes may be another matter.

Although this analysis apparently reduced the importance of the details concerning the Jesus of history, the significance of this appearance in history is by no means diminished. Kierkegaard lays such emphasis upon the actual appearing that it is decisive in his analysis of faith and how men are related to faith. In fact, to explain how men are related to this event Kierkegaard invented a whole new conception of the meaning of fellowship with God or conversion. His new analysis is expressed in his concept of contemporaneity. Faith as the gift of God means that the God who transcends human history and who stands as its judge gives man the condition of believing and saves man from his sins. Since it is God that gives the condition, no one is separated from the saving event. The condition is equally available to all and so all are in this unique sense contemporary with God.

The mention of 'sin' is also a distinctive contribution which Kierkegaard made because throughout the eighteenth and nineteenth centuries the word *sin* had fallen into disuse and unpopularity in philosophical and theological circles. The concept of 'the natural man' recognized something was wrong with modern man, but it did not find something to be so radically wrong that only divine grace could cure it. Man could cure himself. Kierkegaard, however, finds what is wrong with man to be so radical that only divine grace can cure him. For Kierkegaard, man is a sinner and a sinner of his own choice. Kierkegaard raises the question regarding man's sufficiency in a dynamic, new way which reopened the question of sin and also provided a new impulse in recent philosophy : the development of a philosophy of man.

He did not reduce theology to anthropology because of the objective reference to the appearing of God in time. However, Kierkegaard invented a whole new area of theology in his concept of subjectivity. Not since Augustine's *Confessions* or Pascal's *Pensées* have we confronted so full and thorough an analysis of the human subject in its relationship to itself and to grace. For Kierkegaard, salvation and grace occur in an encounter, or as he calls it, in 'the moment'. This subjective encounter is a meeting of two subjects because God is also to be conceived as subject. The whole theological discussion of dialogue in the twentieth century, though emphasized by numerous writers, owes much to the fundamental and radical Kierkegaardian interpretation of the divine-human encounter where the human subject is not the truth, as the *Concluding Unscientific Postscript* maintains, but where, because of sin, the human subject is untruth. In the 'moment', the transcendent God meets man the sinner.

The concept of subjectivity has not only been influential in theology but it has called forth a whole new philosophic point of view commonly called existentialism. This new philosophic point of view finding its point of departure in the existence of the human agent has had ramifications in every discipline and area of humanistic studies. It has created a new venture and a new understanding of art and of literature. It has added dimensions to political, psychological and sociological analysis. It has brought whole new dimensions which had never been considered properly philosophic into the centre of philosophic discussion because for the first time the human being came to be the object of philosophic study.

Historically, philosophy has not been focused on human problems. Rather it has been distracted by the concerns of each particular age. Greek philosophy was concerned with the political problems of the *polis* or city state, an analysis of things in terms of their causes, and in laying the foundations of logic and sciences. Thus, this first great adventure of the human spirit was concerned with everything that man was concerned with, that is, with the objective world but not with man himself. The classical period was one in which man felt that he was master of his fate. The emergence of the Christian philosophy in the Middle Ages was also a distraction, for man, given something new to understand, developed some ingenious systems of great subtlety and power. Yet all the arguments about the Trinity, the First Cause, the proofs for God's existence, the debates over the problem of being in all its many facets, never once raised the problem of the being of man. Man felt wonderfully at home, for though tempted by devils and oppressed by temporal distress, he was able to have hope in the grace of God and comfort in the presence of the Church and the ministry. This world ruled by divine providence was destroyed by the coming of modern science ; for science, it was soon realized, did not need God to guarantee its success. Again, man was distracted from examining the significance of his own being as he went forth to subdue nature for his own practical purposes. However, without the context of God's Providence and grace, man was at a loss to explain why he should bother to do so. Further, as the achievements of science grew even more impressive, man began to feel that this creation of his was now beyond his individual control ; he felt himself to be the victim of history rather than its maker. In this spiritual situation all values inherited from the past became mere slogans and platitudes without meaning for his own existence, and at last man was forced to face the problem of the meaning of his own existence.

Throughout Kierkegaard's work numerous themes which will become prominent in existentialist philosophy appear for the first time as objects of philosophical scrutiny. Such themes as dread, despair, death, hope and subjectivity are themes which he has so pressed upon philosophic minds in the twentieth century that, in the future, philosophy will doubtlessly be unable to forget that existence may be dealt with—subjectively.

Selected Works by Kierkegaard Available in English

The Journals of Søren Kierkegaard, ed. and trans. Alexander Dru, London; Oxford University Press, 1938. Abridged edition, New York: Harper, 1959.*

Søren Kierkegaard: The Last Years: Journals 1853–1855, ed. and tr. Ronald Gregor Smith, New York and Evanston: Harper & Row, 1965.*

Philosophical Fragments, tr. D. F. Swenson. New introduction and commentary by Niels Thulstrup. Translation, revision and commentary tr. by Howard V. Kong. 2nd edn. Princeton University Press, 1962.

The Concept of Dread, tr. with introduction and notes by W. Lowrie. 2nd edn. Princeton University Press, 1957.

Concluding Unscientific Postscript, tr. D. F. Swenson, completed after his death with introduction and notes by W. Lowrie. Princeton University Press for the American Scandinavian Foundation, 1941.

The Sickness unto Death, tr. Walter Lowrie, New York: Doubleday, 1954

The Present Age and Two Minor Ethico-Religious Treatises, tr. Alexander Dru and Walter Lowrie, London and New York: Oxford University Press, 1940*

Purity of Heart is to Will One Thing, tr. with introductory essay by Douglas Steere, 2nd ed., New York: Harper, 1956*

Edifying Discourses, I–IV, tr. David F. Swenson and Lillian Marvin Swenson, Minneapolis: Augsburg, 1943–46*

* Also Fontana Library.